Contents

◀ *Bouldering helps build up stamina and confidence in relative safety*

Introduction

The sport of rock climbing is just one facet of the huge world of mountaineering, and even within this relatively small arena there is a vast amount of knowledge for the novice climber to assimilate. Climbers never cease to learn from their experiences and it is this combination of practical learning and theoretical knowledge that leads to the correct decision being made at critical moments.

Within this book lies enough information for the interested beginner to become an informed participant. This is, however, only a start. It is not possible here to cover all the skills that are necessary to be able to move about the hills with confidence and safety. That requires experience and help from rock climbing friends and colleagues.

The final point to stress is that it is not possible to put the responsibility for your actions onto someone else, be it through the pages of a book or your partner on a climb. You must make your own decisions and then learn to

1

Basic techniques and terms

In order to understand the way in which a pair of climbers might tackle a particular climb up a rock face, it is a good idea to look at the basic system used by climbers world-wide. Assume that two climbers have arrived at the foot of their desired crag, and have chosen to follow a particular *route* which is described in their *guidebook*. They *gear up* and *tie on* to opposite ends of their *climbing rope*. One of them, the *leader*, climbs up the rock until a convenient stopping place, or *stance*, is reached. The *second* then climbs up to join the leader at the stance. The pair continue in the same fashion to the top of the route, using stances to split the route into convenient *pitches*.

The rope between the climbers is not used as an aid to pull on; it is simply a safety device to prevent the climbers falling to the ground should they slip from the rock. Many people unfamiliar with the sport cannot understand how the leader already has the rope in place for him; in fact, he does not.

Looking again at our two climbers – Bob and Sue – once they have tied-on to their rope, Sue decides to *lead* the pitch. She climbs up to the stance at the top of the first pitch, while Bob *pays out* the rope as she moves up. Here she finds a convenient anchor from which to *belay*, or tie herself to (this can be a rock spike, or may be even a tree). Once she is secure, and cannot be pulled from her perch, Bob climbs up to join her, while she *takes in* the rope from above.

Bob and Sue are climbers of similar ability, so when Bob reaches the stance he continues climbing and leads the second pitch. This leapfrogging system is called *leading through*, and it is very efficient, especially on long climbs.

The alternative way of organising the climb would be for Sue to lead all the pitches. When Bob reached her stance he would belay himself and, once he was *safe*, Sue could untie from her anchor and begin to lead the next pitch. In reality, climbers often use a combination of both these systems in order to match the *difficulty* of the pitches to each climber's ability.

Fig. 1 *One of the climbers leads the first pitch of the climb, placing runners as he goes*

2

Fig. 2 *The leader has reached a suitable belay and is taking in excessive rope prior to bringing up his partner*

Fig. 3 *The leader belays the rope as the second climbs up to join him*

Fig. 4 *The original leader now belays the rope for his partner as she leads the second pitch*

3

Calls

It would be unfortunate if one climber started to move up the rock before the other one was safely belayed, and to prevent this happening partners often use an agreed set of *calls* to communicate with each other. Partners who usually climb together will often reduce these to a series of OKs and grunts, but when climbing with comparative strangers it is worth knowing what the other person is doing at all times, especially when the partners are out of sight of each other; misunderstandings have occasionally caused serious accidents. Some of the more universal calls are listed, together with their meanings, below.

Safe or **on belay:** the leader tells the second that she is tied on to an anchor, and that he can stop holding the rope.

Taking in: the leader tells the second that she is pulling up any slack rope that remains between them.

That's me: the second confirms that all the slack has been taken in.

The last few moves of a popular mountain route

Climb when you're ready: the leader tells the second that the rope is being held; he can remove any belay that might be holding him and can prepare to climb.

Climbing: the second confirms that he is about to move.

OK: the leader confirms that everything is in control, and the second can climb up.

A few additional calls are worth noting.

Take in: the second asks the leader to take in any slack that has developed in the rope between them. (Never say 'Take in the slack'.)

Slack: the second asks the leader to pay out some rope. (Using both terms (as above) in the same sentence usually results in the wrong request being granted.)

You've got me: for a variety of potential reasons the weight of one partner is about to be held by the other, so don't pay any rope out.

Once Sue and Bob have reached the top of their route, they *untie* from the rope, and find an easy *way-off* which enables them to walk around to the foot of the crag, where they might pick another route to climb.

The length of climbs vary from area to area, rock type being an important factor. Routes of 200 m are common on mountain crags, while those on small outcrops may be as short as 10 m. Pitch lengths also vary, although they usually involve a *run-out* of between 10 m and 35 m. If the pitches are very long, there is a danger of running out of rope; although 45 m or 50 m ropes are standard, some rope is always taken up by tying-on and belaying.

At a crag where the routes are short, it is likely that a number of routes may be completed by the team, but on a large crag with *multi-pitch* routes one or two climbs would still provide a full day's climbing.

Going climbing

When novices going climbing for the first time ask how to climb, they don't realise that they are simply re-discovering an ability most people mastered before they could walk. Unlike riding a bicycle, for instance, it is not a case of operating some technological invention; rather it is allowing your body to revert to a style of movement that our distant ancestors would have taken for granted. There is no correct body shape or size for a climber. In fact, some of the best rock climbers have been considered short and round or tall and almost anorexic in appearance.

Fitness

A certain degree of overall fitness is certainly a benefit, but the type of strengths that may be vital in some sports may be a drawback to a climber. Perhaps most important are flexibility and agility, both of which may be hampered by excessive amounts of muscle in the wrong places; many good climbers are hopeless at team and ball sports, yet can move up a rockface with consummate ease.

Contemplating just what to do next!

There is really no way of knowing whether people will be good climbers other than by them actually having a go; some will be natural climbers, while others will have to work very hard to achieve the same results. However, both can gain immense satisfaction from their efforts.

Let's return to Bob and Sue on another of their outings. They have parked their car and walked up to the crag they have chosen for the day's climbing. They find a good spot to leave their rucksacks and then wander along the base of the cliff while they consult their guidebook to select a suitable route to climb. Having come to a decision, they return to their rucksacks and sort out their gear.

They put on their harnesses and rock-boots and Bob, who is going to lead the first pitch, sorts out the rack of runners he is going to carry with him on the route. By the time he has sorted everything out, Sue has gone across to the foot of the climb, has uncoiled the rope they are going to use, and has tied on to one end of it. She then places a sling around a boulder and clips it to her harness so that she is not pulled upwards

should Bob fall off the rock. Bob ties on to the other end of the rope and Sue attaches her belay device to the rope near to Bob. She feeds out the rope as he moves upwards, all the time being ready to lock the rope with the belay device if necessary.

Leading skills

The first few metres of the route involve ascending a slab; this requires delicate climbing in which balance and confidence are the climbers' most important assets. A narrow pocket in the rock

A pinch grip hold on a smooth face

A small finger hold on a smooth face

Not all holds work downwards – here a side-pull is being used

allows Bob to place a running belay, or runner, which will prevent him from hitting the ground should he slip from the thin moves at the top of the slab. He chooses a wedge-shaped nut which fits snugly into the pocket and clips it to the rope running down from his waist; aware that he is much safer now, the moves upwards do not seem so bad.

Sue watches attentively, knowing that her reaction is vital should Bob slip from his precarious position. Bob gains a good foot-ledge at the top of the slab and is able to rest for a moment. Climbing is rarely an upward flowing movement: the climber moves in short bursts of activity interspersed with periods of stillness while the next sequence of movement is considered; which hand should go on which hold and which foot should be moved up first? Slab climbing often depends on getting the sequence in the correct order unlike, for example, climbing a crack where each climber may use his or her own version of movements.

Bob is now presented with this very obstacle as the rock above him steepens, although it does provide placements for a number of good sound runners as he gains height. Bob is able to move upwards by combining jamming and laybacking techniques. The crack is much more strenuous to climb than the slab below, and just to stay on the rock requires a great deal of effort.

As the angle of rock changes, the parts of the body that do most of the work change accordingly. On a slab it is

▲ *A finger jam is used in a thinnish crack. The fingers are torqued inside the crack to lock them in place*

A first jam – this is difficult to hold and is often painful ▶

▲ *A hand jam is used in a wider crack – when the hand is placed in the crack and the thumb is pulled down across the palm, it causes the hand to fatten and lock in place*

the legs and feet that take most of the strain, with deft footwork being vital. Those climbers who are not very strong in the arms often find slab climbing the most pleasant. It also provides the opportunity to stand and work out the next moves without expending masses of energy.

As the rock becomes steeper, so the strain on the arms increases and finger strength becomes vital. Obviously, as the difficulty of the climb undertaken is increased, the size of the holds tends to shrink in proportion, and the good ones get further and further apart. On overhanging sections, the whole of the climber's body is involved in the effort to stay attached to the rock; sometimes this is referred to as 'body tension' and it can only be achieved through training combined with a determined build up to this type of route.

Back on the climb, Bob has reached the top of the crack and has pulled himself over onto a good ledge at the bottom corner. A crack in the back of the corner enables runners to be placed and a good belay taken. Sue then removes her belay device from the rope and allows Bob to pull in the remaining slack rope. Bob then attaches the rope to his belay device and Sue is ready to follow the route Bob has taken.

As she climbs up, she removes each of the runners that Bob has placed in the rock, and clips them into the gear loops on her harness. Once she arrives on the belay ledge she is able to collect the unused gear from Bob, who remains

Using a small ledge as a foothold – keep the heel low and don't jump the foot around on the hold

A foothold enhanced by the smearing of the boot onto the rock

Here a foothold is gained by twisting the toes into a crack

attached to the belay, and then consider how she is going to approach the corner above, which is her pitch to lead. The corner looks awkward, but Sue knows that she led a pitch of similar grade the previous weekend and so is confident she can make short work of this one.

Confidence

Just as important as the physical strengths required to succeed on the climb is the right mental approach. Confidence in your ability is essential, as is a good degree of judgement. All the decisions you make during the climb are vital, not just to achieve the objective of completing the climb, but also in making sure that it is never any more dangerous than it needs to be. Yes, climbing is dangerous, but therein lies the thrill and satisfaction of overcoming that danger and reducing it, by skill and judgement, to a tolerable level.

The choices that you make cannot be made by other people, and it is you that has to cope with the consequences of each one; for example, deciding which foot to move first or which crag might have the best weather. Each decision can only be made easier by increasing experience and the application of some common sense. Before climbing with new partners it is as well to remember that, unlike any amount of shiny new equipment, experience and common sense cannot be purchased over the counter in a climbing shop, but they are perhaps the most vital of any climber's attributes.

Success

Sue knows that as long as there are holds on either wall of the corner she will be able to bridge between them and take some of the weight off her arms. She will also be able to place runners while she is in positions that are not too strenuous. There are enough holds to allow the corner to be spanned, and just sufficient runner placements in the crack to allow peace of mind.

Near the top, however, the good holds run out and the last two or three metres look decidedly thin. To make matters worse, the crack in the corner closes and there do not appear to be any more runner possibilities for some way.

Novices often don't understand just which shapes or formations of rock can be used as holds. When there are no obvious footholds, boots can be smeared onto the slightest rugosity; handholds can be made of any slight edge, be it horizontal, sideways on or even upside-down. A crack of any kind always contains the possibility of a hold, even if jamming fingers, hands or arms into it is necessary.

A couple of diagonal creases allow a purchase for the fingers, allowing Sue to stand up and reach small finger holds. This is it, the crux of the climb; holding her breath, she reaches higher. But she's not quite there; she can't reach a good hold. Steadying herself, she moves her feet a little higher and reaches up again.

Suddenly it is all over and the holds seem to grow in size as she finishes the corner and pulls over onto the top of the crag. She finds good belays and settles down to hold Bob's rope, knowing that although he has a longer reach his big feet will make the footholds even harder to smear onto.

Although your partner is there on the other end of the rope, there is no team to satisfy and no fixture to win. There is simply a challenge to be met; success comes through your skill and judgement and a feeling of satisfaction is experienced when both partners need and trust in each other for that climb. There is no one to tell you which route you must do or that you must go to a particular crag. You have the freedom to make those choices for yourself, and to set the targets you hope to achieve. This is what sets climbing apart from so many sports and why so many strong individualists partake in such a great pastime.

Fig. 5 *A typical modern rock climbing boot*

Equipment

As I have suggested earlier, it is important for the novice climber to understand that it is a combination of ability and judgement, rather than shiny new equipment that makes climbing safe and enjoyable. It is perfectly possible to go bouldering on gritstone outcrops with no equipment at all, but having said this, a certain amount of gear will make the climbing experience rather more pleasurable for most participants.

The sheer volume and variety of equipment that presents itself to an inexperienced climber entering a climbing gear shop will be totally overwhelming, and it is quite easy to end up paying a good deal of money for superfluous items. The following are items of equipment presented in the order a novice might expect to purchase them.

Climbing boots or shoes

These are the one exception to the rule that there is no gear that will actually make you climb better. The modern boot boasts an extremely sticky rubber sole, rather like that of a Formula One racing car tyre, and provides a measure of support across the sole of the foot, thus enabling the wearer to stand on tiny holds with relative ease. There are many different makes of boot: some are substantially stiffened to provide the foot with lots of support, while others are constructed in a way that allows the foot more flexibility to smear the edge of the sole onto small sloping holds.

Shoes are, in effect, cut down versions of the boots which allow for greater movement at the ankle, though this is achieved at the expense of some support.

Virtually all boots have a lacing system that extends right down to the toes, to give a snug fit. However, a few designs may prove uncomfortable for some climbers due to excessive narrowing of the toe shape. This is to enable cracks and small pockets to be more easily used as footholds. Slippers have also become fashionable lately; these very soft and often slip-on rock shoes have the advantage of providing unrivalled 'feel' of the rock, but they provide minimal support.

With such a wide range of footwear, perhaps the best way to choose a boot is by quizzing friends with similarly shaped feet and begging a quick trial of the boots they recommend.

Helmet

The danger of damage to the head, especially the brain, from falls and, even more importantly, from falling rocks suggests that it would be sensible to wear a helmet whenever on a crag. Modern designs and construction techniques have allowed helmets to be lightweight, yet extremely strong. In fact, carbon-fibre reinforced plastic and kevlar reinforced glass-fibre helmets can far exceed the requirements of the current safety standards. Helmets are certainly much more 'wearable' in general than they were in previous years and, given the continual catalogue of head injuries on mountain crags, they should be considered an important item of equipment.

Harness

A comfortable harness can be advantageous. In some European countries, full-body harnesses are often worn, but in Britain it is rare to see anything other than a sit-harness being used. This consists of two parts: a strong waist belt and a pair of leg loops. The parts may, according to the model and make, be detachable from each another or they may be combined into one single unit. Both sections are made from nylon webbing and are usually padded for extra comfort.

Fig. 6 *A lightweight, but very strong, plastic helmet*

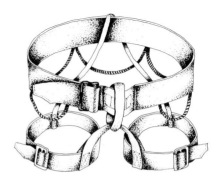

Fig. 7 *A sit-harness showing all the essential features of good design*

The best designs are those which have the following features: a waist belt which, when the harness is put on, makes a complete and substantial circle around the body; a relatively foolproof through-and-back buckle so that any error in fastening is immediately obvious; adjustable leg-loops so that different thicknesses of clothing can be accommodated while still allowing a snug fit; and a strong, reinforced belay loop at the front of the harness which is integral with the waist belt and also, if possible, with the leg-loops.

11

The harness may also include gear-loops for clipping runners, etc. into, but these may not be important if a bandolier is to be used. It is imperative that any harness you might consider purchasing comes complete with comprehensive instructions for its use, especially the tying-in of the climbing rope, and that these are followed precisely whenever the harness is used.

Belay device

Having purchased a harness, it should not be considered complete without a belay device kept permanently with it. In the event of a fall, these devices enable the belayer to grip or belay the rope without having to wrap it around his body (the latter practice always entails wearing full arm-covering clothing and usually gloves as well).

The most popular device is the Sticht plate, which has a spring to help prevent the rope from jamming unnecessarily, although the Tuber, a tapered tube as the name suggests, is rapidly gaining popularity.

Each of these devices should be used in conjunction with a large screw-gate

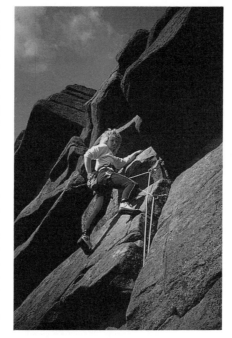

Well-protected climbing through a series of small gritstone overhangs

karabiner, ideally of a pear-shaped design for ease, and attached to the strong belay loop at the front of the har-

ness. They can be kept to hand at the rear of the harness when not in use.

Often climbers are seen carrying a figure of eight descendeur (see glossary) in addition to the belay device. This is usually unnecessary, as the Sticht plate or Tuber are quite adequate for abseils, except long, multiple descents where a larger heat-sink is important.

Rope

A rope is the one item of equipment that most people always associate with climbing. However, it is still only a single link in the safety chain that allows a climber to fall off occasionally without hitting the ground!

Constructed from a core of continuous nylon filaments encased in a tough woven sheath, a modern kernmantle climbing rope is extremely strong, yet light, flexible and somewhat elastic. The elasticity is present in order to absorb some of the energy generated by a fall and enables the climber to be brought to a gentle stop rather than to a traumatic, abrupt halt which an incredibly strong, for example wire rope, would provide. It also has the effect of transferring less load onto the

An awkward chimney pitch relents only after some trying moves

equipment and anchors to which the rope is attached.

The standard dimensions for a rope are either a single 11 mm diameter by 45 m or 50 m length or two 9 mm diameter by 45 m or 50 m lengths. The latter allows greater protection, although at the price of slightly more complex ropework.

When in use, 'do nots' include standing on the rope (when grit particles can enter the core), running the rope over sharp edges under load (by far the most common cause of rope damage), and contact with chemicals (petrol, battery acid etc.). Chemical contact is the most common cause of total rope failure. If you suspect this may have happened to your rope, throw it away: your life is more valuable than any rope!

Ropes, like helmets and some karabiners, are subject to UIAA (see glossary) standards which have made it impossible to buy a sub-standard rope, although there is still a good variety in the handling characteristics of each make. I would recommend that the novice looks for a tightly-sheathed 'hard' type of rope, because the resistance to wear and minimal drag through runners more than compensate for the reduced 'nice' feel of softer and more supple ropes. When your life relies fairly often on the soundness of a rope, it would be foolish even to consider buying a second-hand one, the history of which is unknown.

Miscellanea

Once the basics have been obtained, the novice can start to build up a rack of gear for use when leading. This will include slings, nuts (both rocks and hexentrics), karabiners (both screwgates for belays and snap-gates for runners) and perhaps the odd friend (or similar device) and some micro-wires.

When climbing with a regular partner it should be possible to pool each other's gear to provide a comprehensive selection and each can provide one 9 mm by 50 m rope to form a double rope for climbing with. Other gear might include a chalk bag and prusik loops which enable the rope to be ascended and various ropework rescue systems to be constructed. Chalk can be used on indoor climbing walls, when bouldering and on high standard climbs, but its use on easy climbs is considered by many climbers to be unethical and even offensive.

Some of the most popular forms of

clothing are tracksuit pants and fibre-pile or thermo-fleece tops, a combination which provides warmth while allowing great flexibility of movement. However, jumpers and loose trousers of any description are fine to start with.

The safety chain

The main principle of modern climbing ropework is that only one person in the party moves at a time. Obviously the person at most risk of a fall is the leader and, as we have seen, he 'sews' his rope to the rock with runners as he climbs upwards. In the event of a fall, it is vital that each link of the safety chain is strong enough to withstand the forces placed upon it. The chain is as follows:

the falling leader
his harness
the tying-on knot
the rope
one or more runners
the second's belay device
the second's harness and knots
the belay anchors.

It is important that the leader places at least one runner as soon as possible after leaving the belay ledge on a multi-pitch climb. Without a runner in place, the force of any fall directly onto the belay is much greater and is much more likely to result in failure of the belay and possible disastrous consequences.

A large selection of nuts, both wedges and hexentrics, Friend-type camming devices and quick draws. Although a climber might possess this amount of hardware, only a selection suitable for the chosen route would be taken on the climb

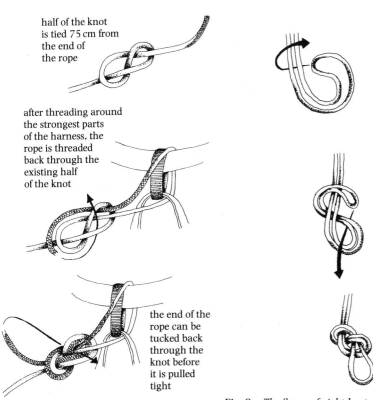

half of the knot is tied 75 cm from the end of the rope

after threading around the strongest parts of the harness, the rope is threaded back through the existing half of the knot

the end of the rope can be tucked back through the knot before it is pulled tight

Fig. 8 *The figure-of-eight knot used to tie on to a harness*

Fig. 9 *The figure-of-eight knot tied on a bight of rope to form a strong loop*

Knots

Figure-of-eight knot

The figure-of-eight is by far the safest knot for tying-on to the climbing rope. It is a follow-through knot and it is easy to spot an error if it is tied incorrectly. The end of the rope either tucks back through the knot or is used to make an extra locking hitch. In addition, the figure-of-eight tied on a bight, or loop, of rope is often used to form part of a belay system, as is the figure-of-eight tie-back knot.

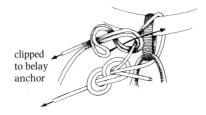

clipped to belay anchor

Fig. 10 *Use a figure-of-eight knot to tie back the rope after clipping in a belay point*

15

Clove hitch

The clove hitch comes into its own when using double ropes, being a quick and simple way of attaching the ropes to the runners making up the belay. It is not quite as strong as the figure-of-eight, so it should not be used as the single anchoring knot.

Fig. 11 *The clove hitch used to tie into a karabiner*

Double fisherman's knot

This is the best knot for joining two ropes, for either an abseil or the ends of the rope loop of a sling or nut runner.

Fig. 12 *The double fisherman's knot used to join two ropes*

Tape knot

The only other knot that is important is the tape (or water) knot. This is used whenever two ends of tape are tied together, and it is another follow-through knot.

All knots in climbing rope or tape tend to work loose. It is therefore crucial that they are pulled tight when tied, and are regularly checked for slackness.

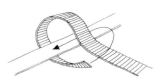

Fig. 13 *The tape knot used to join nylon webbing*

Runners

These come in so many varieties that it would be impossible for the leader actually to climb if all of them were carried, so I shall look at the basic types.

Nuts come in three types: *wedges,*

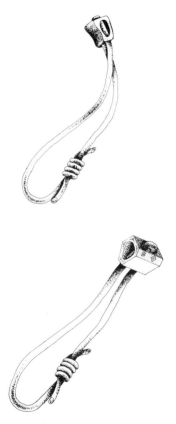

◀ **Fig. 14** *A wedge-shaped nut ('Rock') on rope*

are best hung on rope; and *micro-wires*, which are very tiny nuts and are usually soldered directly onto the wire. They work where no other protection will, but only if the rock is strong enough.

Friends are still probably the best of the camming devices and are designed to work in parallel-sided cracks. They cover a range of widths in each size.

Fig. 16 *A tiny brass wedge, or micro-nut, on wire*

which are exactly what the name implies (the most popular variety are those with curved faces which are referred to by their trade name of rocks), the larger sizes being hung on rope, the smaller ones, on steel wire; *hexentrics*, which are more tubular in shape than wedges, are designed to offer three different widths of placement per size, and

Fig. 15 *An hexentric nut on rope*

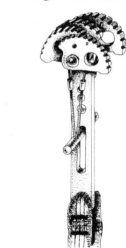

Fig. 17 *A 'Friend' camming device with sewn tape sling attached*

17

Slings are loops, either sewn or knotted, of tape or rope which can be used over spikes of rock, around boulders or in threads to make runners. Tape slings tend to be better at staying on spikes without the loop rolling off.

Fig. 18 *A tape sling, in use as a belay on a rock spike*

Each runner requires a snap-gate *karabiner* with which to clip it into the climbing rope, except wires which require a quick-draw (a very short sling with a karabiner at each end) in order to prevent it being levered out of the placement. When using a single rope, many of the runners will have to be extended

Fig. 19 *A snap-gate karabiner shown with the gate open*

Fig. 20 *A screw-gate karabiner, for use on belays, shown with the gate locked shut*

Fig. 21 *A quick-draw with a snap-gate karabiner at each end*

in order to prevent excessive rope drag; this is not so important when using double ropes.

Watch the way an experienced climber always seems to select the correct size of runner first time – this is simply through practice. Borrow a rack of gear and attempt to place runners at the base of the crag, then try to get your efforts examined critically by someone more experienced than you.

Belay systems

It is unfortunate that the word 'belay' is used to describe so many slightly different things. It will be used here to describe the way the second is attached to anchors that prevent him from being pulled from his stance. The 'belayer' is the person thus anchored and the 'belay device' is used to grip the rope running up to the lead climber.

Only if the anchor is very substantial (e.g. a large boulder or tree) should a single belay be employed; otherwise, two should be considered a minimum and the poorer each one is, the greater the total number of anchors there should be.

The forces involved, should the leader fall, can be very large, so each anchor should be examined critically. The slightest movement or hollowness should automatically infer doubt. Each anchor should be tied statically and individually to the front of the belayer's harness using screw-gate karabiners and figure-of-eight knots or clove hitches. Back to back snap-gate karabiners can be used as a substitute for screw-gates. Never should all the

Fig. 22 *Here a leader brings the second up to his belay. If the leader stands tight from the anchors, the potential force (in the event of a slip by the second) should be body weight only*

Fig. 23 *In this case, the leader has fallen off, with no runners in place. This is the most serious type of fall and will result in maximum forces being transmitted to the belayer and the anchors. This situation should be avoided if at all possible*

anchors just be clipped unknotted into the same loop of rope. Remember that once the leader has placed a runner, any fall will result in an upward pull on the belay. You have to ask yourself whether this would lift out the anchors.

Try to stand in sight of your partner, but make sure that this is in line with the predicted pull and the belay, otherwise a nasty sideways jerk will result. Once fastened to the anchors, you should lean away slightly, putting your

The belayer has used a figure-of-eight tie-back to form a belay system, with a sling around a tree as a single substantial anchor. A 'Tuber' belay device is being used to grip the rope running down to the climber's partner

Fig. 24 *Although the leader has fallen, he has taken the precaution of placing a number of runners. This considerably reduces the load on the belayer and anchors, although the force acts upwards rather than downwards*

weight on the anchors to ensure that, in the event of a leader fall, none of the anchors are shock-loaded, which would increase the probability of failure. If you don't have enough faith in the anchors to lean tight from them, they cannot be expected to hold a fall! If the anchors are good, then trust them; if they aren't good, find some better ones.

Belay devices

The belay device should be attached to the belay loop at the front of the harness, and preferably to the tie-in loop of rope as well, with a screw-gate karabiner. Both the Sticht plate and Tuber devices work in the event of a fall by forcing the rope into some tight turns through them. It is thus held by the friction this generates. They are moder-

When using double ropes, each can be fastened to the anchor with clove hitches. Note how the climber is standing tight on the belays to prevent any unnecessary shock loading

Fig. 25 *A Sticht plate belay device in use on the front of a harness*

ately foolproof to use, but the detailed instructions accompanying each device when sold should be thoroughly learned.

The rope should be payed out in such a way that the leader can move upwards without it becoming tight (thereby pulling him off). Having said that, there should not be so much slack that the leader would fall some way before the rope came tight. If the rope has been carefully piled on one side, so that it pays out from the top, tangles will be minimised. When using double ropes, one rope often has to be payed out as the other is taken in. With a little practice this is quite easy to do.

Double ropes

Using two 9 mm diameter ropes instead of a single rope has the advantages of: allowing the leader to protect better both himself and the second when the line of the route wanders around on the rockface; causing much less rope drag from runners; making belaying simpler; and allowing much longer abseils should retreat become necessary.

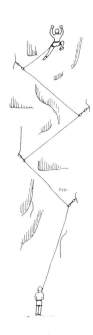

Fig. 26 *A single rope sometimes causes considerable rope drag, which will be experienced by the leader*

Fig. 27 *A double rope system allows the same number of runners to be employed, but with much less rope drag than in a single rope system*

Fig. 28 *A top* ▶
roping system using
a strong tree belay
and screw-gate
karabiners

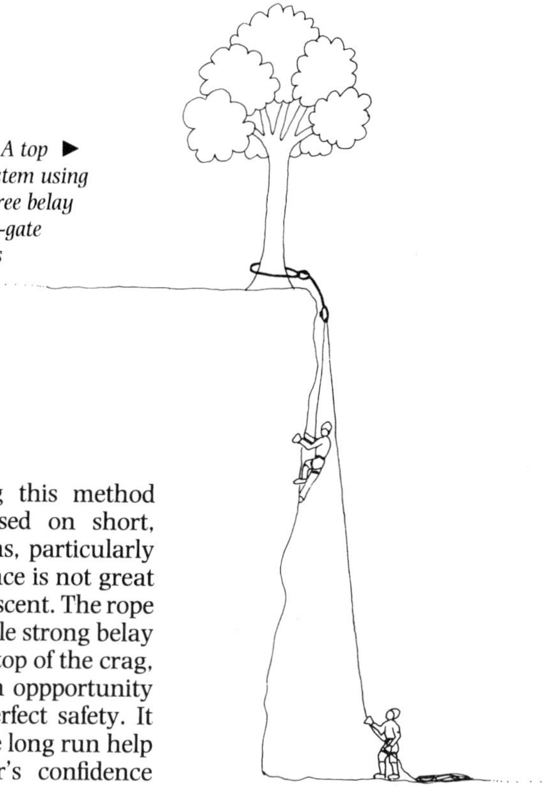

Top roping

It is worth mentioning this method which is commonly used on short, difficult outcrop problems, particularly where ability or experience is not great enough to justify a solo ascent. The rope is arranged with a suitable strong belay acting as a pulley at the top of the crag, and gives the climber an oppportunity to try hard moves in perfect safety. It does not, however, in the long run help to increase the climber's confidence when leading.

Abseiling

This German word (often shortened to 'ab' or 'abbing') is used to describe the method of descending a crag by means of a rope. Basically, the rope is doubled, the middle being passed around a suitable anchor, and the ends are thrown down to the ground. The climber slides, with control, down the ropes by means of a friction device or descendeur. The ropes can then be retrieved by pulling on one of the ends and thus unravelling it from around the anchor.

The technique is most often used when there is no easy way down from the climb, or as an approach to sea cliff climbs. The French term 'rappel' (or 'rap') has also become popular.

Most modern harnesses have a permanent loop at the front to which to attach the friction device, usually a figure-of-eight descendeur, although many other devices are available. Sticht plates are often used in this way, although they do not provide as good a heat-sink as the more chunky descendeurs.

A long 'free' abseil

Minimising the risks

It is unfortunate that this climbing technique has been over-popularised by the media and by charity/publicity events in which participants bounce spectacularly down crags and walls on ropes anchored to perfect belays, because it is potentially the most dangerous activity most climbers ever undertake. It is often the one part of a day's climbing when total reliance is placed on the gear and anchors; unless you are in the habit of constantly falling off, the efficiency of the rest of your ropework techniques are often never tested for real. Many climbers, both novices and internationally renowned mountaineers alike, have been killed whilst abseiling, so it is worth considering the following points:

Are the anchors good enough?

If an anchor fails, you are in deep trouble. Large, hefty trees do not abound on ledges, and real abseils are often from less than perfect anchors. The anchor should be the best available, and must be backed up by another if there is any doubt about its strength. Replace any tape or rope left by other climbers when abseiling from fixed gear such as pitons; a few pence worth of gear is no loss when compared with staying alive. Abseil as smoothly as possible: every jerk or bounce puts extra load on the anchors.

Are the ropes long enough?

If they are not, there is a good chance of either sliding off the end of them or being stuck in mid-air if you have to abseil over an overhang. Before throwing the ends of the rope down, check that the middle is tied into the anchor! Tie a knot in the ends of the ropes and always remain in control of your speed of descent.

Is there a chance of stonefall?

Falling rocks might cut the ropes or hit a climber and knock him unconscious, particularly if he is not wearing a helmet. So, take care not to knock stones down onto yourself when swinging about on the rope.

Will the rope jam around the anchor?

The first climber down should check to see that the ropes will run through the anchor smoothly. If the ropes jam either at the anchor or as they are pulled down, do not try to climb up them unbelayed; they have a nasty habit of coming loose again once the climber is committed to them. The first climber should also clear any tangles and knots on the way down. Never get into the situation in which the ends of the rope are left jammed above the descending climber.

Is your harness done up properly?

There is no second chance once you have stepped over the edge. The descender should be attached to the correct part of your harness with a screwgate karabiner. This prevents the device twisting out of the karabiner during the descent.

These thoughts are not designed to put you off from abseiling, but rather to make sure every abseil is approached with the right degree of caution. If you are going to abseil for the first time, don't be afraid to ask for a safety rope. Until you understand what you are doing, it would be wise not to make your first mistake your last.

Ethics

Climbing is a very strange sport in some ways. It doesn't have a set of rules laid down by a governing body and climbers can go about their pastime in any manner they wish, provided it does not affect the rest of the climbing community. Having said that, there exists a complicated and constantly changing code that suggests what constitutes acceptable behaviour and what does not. This can be condensed to two basic ideas: firstly, that wherever possible the rock should be left in the same state after an ascent as it was in before the climb; and, secondly, that however anyone ascends a route, they should tell the truth about it.

Care of the crag

As the use of pitons for protection of the leader died out in favour of nut runners, so the concept of leaving the rock as it was found became an extremely important one. It would be fair to say that the most heinous act a climber can commit

is to chip holds or deliberately alter the rock in some way.

While the removal of loose rock prior to a first ascent is acceptable in most

A serious lead on a steep slate slab

places, a climber's wilful alteration of the rock reveals his lack of feeling for the rock and his probable inability to ascend it in its virgin state. The majority of climbers would rather admit defeat and leave it for someone better to climb. To be found guilty of having smashed the rock into submission holds no greater shame.

The current dismay at the proliferation of bolt runner protection is a direct result of this ideal. The placement of bolts means that the rock is irreversibly altered. While they have been accepted on a very few crags, notably limestone and slate, their use is universally reviled in all other areas; indeed, the few misguidedly placed bolts on granite and other volcanic rocks have been quickly removed, and the protagonists shunned.

Sport climbing

During the early '80s, the indiscriminate use of bolt runners on the continent, especially in France, led to French climbers having a much higher technical skill level than their British counterparts. This had a deep influence on a number of climbers, and has been responsible for a divergence of British climbing into two schools of thought during the last few years.

One branch has taken the bolt-protected path, and this has fostered the development of sport climbing. The climbs are almost totally protected by bolt runners, and involve merely a great amount of gymnastic skill and effort, with little risk or adventure. It may take days or even months of practice before a climber solves the puzzle of how to complete the route. It has led to the establishing of climbing competitions which are held exclusively on indoor artificial walls, perhaps in an attempt to provide the excitement missing from this type of route. Sport climbing has enabled leading British sports climbers to equal technically, and even overtake, their counterparts worldwide.

Real climbing

The other branch has pursued the traditional British approach and has continued to use predominantly nut protection on new routes, with a resurgence of new routes being led without previous cleaning or inspection. This now means that many of the world's most serious routes are in Britain, and among the British climbing fraternity are some of the best exponents of skill, judgement and nerve within the sport.

At present, the majority of climbers would wish climbing in Britain to remain just the way it is. There is simply not enough rock to allow bolts to be smashed into a large proportion of it.

Telling the truth

The second of our basic ideas is slightly more aesthetic than physical. Most climbers have a 'hit list' of climbs they would like to do, and these are often just at the limit of their ability. Occasionally the routes turn out to be a little too difficult; may be a lack of confidence or simply not feeling good enough on the day, is the cause, and the climber either falls off or perhaps pulls on a runner.

It would be wrong for that same climber to go away and tell his friends that he had completed the climb with no problem. It would certainly not win their respect when the truth eventually came to light (as it invariably does), and it could even tempt others into territory beyond their limits. In the very worst cases, climbers have lied about new routes they claimed to have ascended. The truth has always emerged and those individuals have been ridiculed and their other achievements cast into doubt.

These ethical concepts are not difficult to grasp; they are merely the application of a little common sense, respect for the rock and an awareness of the original values of the sport.

Jamming and bridging on steep granite

Access and conservation

Almost all of the climbing sites in Britain are situated on private property and access to climb on these crags must never be taken for granted. Even land in National Parks is privately owned, be it the National Trust or individual farmers.

With the selling off of large areas of public land, and the decreasing support for hill farmers, climbers will in the future be under greater and greater pressure either to pay for, or to refrain from taking part in, their sport. This can only be avoided if climbers are seen to take some responsibility in caring for the countryside and helping prevent unnecessary damage to the landscape. Although climbers of mountain crags are assured of relatively free access to climb, many more urban crags could easily be lost if climbers fail to realise that their respect and co-operation are critical. It is vital that the access directions recorded in guidebooks are

Bridging across a corner keeps the climber's weight on his feet and so reduces the strain on the arms

accurately followed and that the Country Code is observed.

Disputes involving landowners and climbers are sometimes resolved by the mediation of the British Mountaineering Council (BMC), and to this end many guidebook publishers donate a small levy, applied on guidebook sales, to the BMC Access and Conservation Fund. The money is used to finance the erection of stiles, repair of fences and display of access details, etc.

Getting started and getting better

In the past, many now famous climbers began climbing with friends who did not know what they were doing; most of them were lucky enough to survive to an age when they knew better. Many youngsters today experience rock climbing and abseiling on courses at outdoor pursuit centres or with the various youth organisations, but there is often difficulty in finding a way to progress outside these situations. For adults the chance to partake in the sport can seem even more remote.

There are, however, a number of ways to become involved, although a little luck in meeting the right people is

◀ *Laybacking a corner is a strenuous undertaking, but it can be adopted when there are no footholds*

always handy. Traditionally, it has always been supposed that getting hold of some kind of rope, going out and doing what you imagine to be the right thing is the best way to start. That's fine for natural survivors, but we now know so much about techniques, gear and, more importantly, how to use them correctly, that it is really worth finding out how to do everything safely.

Clubs

Joining a climbing trip with friends who already climb is a good beginning. You will certainly find out if the sport is to your taste. They will probably have enough equipment with them for you to borrow a harness, helmet and may be even rock-boots. Best of all, you can simply have a go.

Your friends may belong to a climbing or mountaineering club. Many clubs welcome new members and have a structure that ensures novices receive some kind of guidance until they understand what they are doing. These clubs exist in towns and cities all over the country and not just in climbing areas. Their locations can be obtained from the

A mantle shelf move can be made to gain a ledge when few holds exist above and below. Note the hands pressing downwards on the ledge

BMC or from the club pages of mountaineering magazines.

Clubs often own huts in climbing areas that provide the base for weekend forays. Visits further afield are often organised and regular meetings and lectures are arranged during the winter.

It is well worth reading a book or two about the use of equipment, and taking note of the information; even the most benevolent of friends will run out of patience if you don't contribute anything at all to the day's proceedings.

Courses

Many people are just not gregarious and may be apprehensive about the 'club'-type organisations. So, a better approach for them might be to go on a course of some kind (there are very few climbers, in fact, who wouldn't learn something from a good instructional session).

High quality courses are available from many sources. Those directed by members of the Association of Mountain Instructors (AMI) or British Association of Mountain Guides (BAMG) should guarantee adequate safety with adventure standards. Again, the BMC can provide information about these courses. Some education authorities also maintain their own outdoor education centres. Your local school, youth club or education authority can provide details of their facilities.

Practice

Bouldering

The best way to improve your performance is simply to go climbing; not up big routes, but on large rocks and the first few metres of the crags – this is called bouldering. Either on your own, or with a group of friends, it is possible to work out small routes, or problems, up the rock and then to try to climb them.

Another way of approaching the activity is to attempt traverses of a crag, i.e. to climb sideways across the bottom of the crag, just above the ground.

Traversing is often used to build up reserves of stamina. Even if you only usually climb, for example, 'Very Difficult' routes, it is perfectly possible to complete moves and problems of 'Very Severe' grade and above. After regular sessions of bouldering, your climbing

When climbing a slab, the body should be kept well away from the rock, with the weight over the feet

Wall climbing puts constant strain on the arms, and automatically pulls the body closer to the rock

Buildering

In cities you can often find walls and buildings that are of a suitable texture on which to practise. You must, of course, discover the owners of these before attempting any climbing. Having

standard should increase accordingly. However, this is assuming that a crag is easily available, which may not always be the case.

A well-featured rock face allows both cracks and face holds to be used

When the rock face is less featured, it may force the climber to ascend a crack without help from face holds around it. Here both hands and both feet must be jammed into the fissure

done that, buildering, as it is termed, provides some unique and interesting problems, especially in crag-free areas.

Artificial walls

Even in areas well provided for in terms of natural crags, the winter months bring weather that makes training outdoors just impossible. During the last ten years there has been a huge increase in the numbers of artificial climbing walls available to climbers for training.

These are purpose-built structures covered in holds and often situated in sports centres or similar establishments.

They are made from a variety of materials and the best ones have holds that are similar to those found on real cliffs. The walls are often situated near multi-gym facilities which are found useful by many climbers. However, it is worth remembering that it is only worth improving the performance of muscles that are actually going to be used in climbing. For example, jogging might be beneficial for general fitness, but it is of little direct use in climbing.

Many climbers have constructed their own improvised climbing walls at home. These vary from commercially available finger-boards, which can be placed above a door frame, to extensive areas of loft or cellar with home-made holds or even pre-formed bolt-on holds of the type used on large sports-centre type walls.

The only problem that has recently emerged from the use of these walls is severe joint and tendon damage that can occur when exercises have been continued through the body's natural pain barriers. The saying 'no pain, no gain' is true, but the pain associated with increasing stamina is distinctly different from that indicating damage to tissue and bone. To recognise this difference is vital if serious physiological problems in later years are to be avoided.

Interestingly, climbing walls have led to comparatively novice climbers being able to climb at quite high standards on their first real climbing session. The approach is totally different from the traditional way of becoming involved in climbing, which progressed from hill-walking, through easy climbs to harder routes, and which had the advantage of not putting comparative novices in situations where their experience and resourcefulness did not match up to the technical standard of the route they had embarked upon.

Climbing walls provide a great way of staying in shape over the winter and can certainly help towards an increase of strength and stamina for the next season. Details of all the artificial walls in Britain are held by the BMC.

Fitness

In recent years, climbers have become increasingly aware of their general fitness and health, assuming, probably correctly, that all-round care of their

bodies will result in an improved climbing performance. Non-specific training often includes careful examination of diet and the intake of various drugs such as caffeine, nicotine and alcohol, although the image of climbers as addicts of huge greasy meals will take a few years yet to dispel. Other more specific training regimes often include stretching exercises. These are designed to keep the whole body supple in spite of strength gains, which generally tend to make the body stiffer and less flexible.

◀ *Reaching up for holds on an American sandstone wall*

Guidebooks, grades and where to climb

The first team to climb up a rockface by a particular way are said to have ascended a new route. These routes are named, graded and recorded in magazines, club journals or other places where *new routes books* are kept (often cafés frequented by climbers). These records are eventually incorporated into guidebooks which detail all the routes in each given area.

The way in which a climb is described has become standardised as illustrated in the following fictional example.

**The Overhanging Wall 50 m Hard Very Severe (1957)
A fine strenuous climb up the obvious steep wall.
1 35 m 5a. Start in the centre of the wall and boldly follow good holds to a small ledge at 20 m. The crack splitting the steep ground above is followed, with good protection, to a large ledge with good belays.

2 15 m 4b. The groove above leads more easily to the top.

Let's look briefly at what this all means. The two stars at the beginning indicate that this is a very good quality climb. (The scale of stars runs from none to three, with only the most outstanding climbs receiving a coverted three stars.) The name of the route is that given to it by the first ascentionists and may be descriptive, humorous or inspiring; the possibilities are endless.

Next comes the total length of the route, measured in climbed distance rather than vertical height gained. The grade of the route then follows and this gives an overall idea of the difficulty of this particular way up the cliff. The figure in brackets records the year the route was first climbed.

Beneath the first line is usually a short note about the route in general, followed by a more detailed description of each pitch. In this example, face climbing on good holds is followed by a steeper section of crack climbing, with an easy groove to finish off with.

A climber is placing a runner on his first lead

Grades

Looking at the grade in more detail we find it is usually taken from the following scale.

Grade	Abbreviation	Usual technical pitch grades
Moderate	Mod	—
Difficult	Diff	—
Very Difficult	V Diff	—
Severe	S	—
Hard Severe	HS	4a, 4b
Very Severe	VS	4a, 4b, 4c
Hard Very Severe	HVS	5a, 5b
Extremely Severe	E1	5b, 5c
Extremely Severe	E2	5b, 5c
Extremely Severe	E3	5c, 6a
Extremely Severe	E4	5c, 6a, 6b
Extremely Severe	E5	6a, 6b, 6c
Extremely Severe	E6	6a, 6b, 6c
Extremely Severe	E7	6b, 6c, 7a
Extremely Severe	E8	6b, 6c, 7a

The scale is open-ended and harder climbs are being claimed all the time, although it always takes a few repeat ascents of a new climb before the grade is properly established. Different areas of the country sometimes use additional sub-grades such as Hard Very Difficult or Mild Very Severe.

The adjective grade describes the overall difficulty of the climb, including rock quality, protection, degree of exposure and how sustained the technical difficulty may be (an E number simply shows that the climb is in the Extreme grade). The technical pitch grade should describe the hardest climbing moves encountered as if the climber was on a top-rope.

One rock type may seem quite different in gradings to another until the new type has been fully understood; big exposed mountain climbs are often technically easier, for a given grade, than short quarry type routes, although they may seem just as difficult at the time. Very short routes, usually climbed solo, are often simply given a technical grade, and climbs that are protected solely by in-situ bolt runners are increasingly being graded on the French scale of difficulty (see 'Ethics').

Climbing conversation sometimes seems to consist totally of argument about grades and it is easy to lose sight of the fun of climbing beneath the striving to advance one's personal climbing standard. The grading system merely attempts to provide a route that will challenge, but not overwhelm, the climber. Climbing is supposed to be an enjoyable sport and remember: there will always be someone who is climbing better than you are; however, they might not be having such a good time!

Guidebooks

Guidebooks are published by various climbing clubs, the British Mountaineering Council and other specialist publishers. They generally include detailed route descriptions, crag diagrams and a comprehensive quality assessment. They may seem expensive at first – certainly to buy every guidebook in Britain would cost several hundred pounds – but they are produced virtually at cost, often by a team of volunteer writers.

Definitive guidebooks list every climb in a particular area and are generally purchased by climbers who intend to visit that area quite often. *Selected climbs* guidebooks list, in their authors' opinion, only the very best climbs in any given area, and provide a better buy for areas only visited occasionally by the climber. A number of glossy coffee-table tomes offer essays by various authors on the outstanding or *classic* climbs to be found all over Britain, and provide a great source of inspiration. A good climbing equipment shop should be able to provide a selection of guidebooks and be able to obtain the most up-to-date edition for any area in the country, not to mention the world. Many bookshops and libraries also have a comprehensive mountaineering and rock climbing section.

Climbing areas

Virtually every region of Britain has some area of climbing potential, but there are a number that stand out in terms of quality and sheer quantity of climbs available. Scotland has a huge variety of climbing areas, from the well-known mountain regions of Glencoe, Ben Nevis, the Cairngorms and Skye to the highest crags in Britain rising from the sea in the Orkneys; the Old Man of Hoy is probably the best-known sea cliff climb in the country.

The Lake District provides many mountain crags in beautiful settings, as well as limestone valley crags in the southern area. Northumberland and Lancashire are dotted with natural sandstone outcrops and quarries which are tremendously popular, although these are more than rivalled by Derbyshire and Yorkshire which have numerous natural gritstone edges up on the moors and large limestone crags in the dales. The area between Sheffield, Manchester and Stoke-on-Trent, the Peak, is probably the most popular, with literally thousands of climbers to be seen on the rocks each weekend.

Snowdonia offers a considerable variety of climbing venues, from mountain crags to slate quarries, from roadside limestone outcrops to breathtaking sea cliffs. Further south, Pembroke now has a huge number of sea cliff climbs, mostly on steep limestone. The Bristol area boasts inland limestone crags, while the south west is blessed with all sorts of moorland and sea cliff climbing, the Land's End area being the spiritual home of this latter branch of the sport. Even the south east has a few, understandably very popular, sandstone outcrops to the south of London.

Modern British climbers often go abroad to sample climbing in other countries. France, Italy and Spain are hugely popular locations, while further afield Australia and America are now visited by the roving rock climber. The sport has become a passport to friendships all around the world.

The British Mountaineering Council

The British Mountaineering Council, more commonly known simply as the BMC, is the representative body of British rock climbers and mountaineers. It is a democratic body made up of individual members and affiliated mountaineering clubs in England and Wales (Scotland has a similar, but smaller, body: The Mountaineering Council of Scotland (MC of S). It provides a local, national and international voice for British climbers.

Services and areas of expertise include access work, liaison with conservationists, equipment testing, international rescue insurance, conference organisation, competition climbing, mountain training and guidebook production.

Although it is obviously not compulsory for climbers to be members of the BMC, many feel it is vitally important to support the national body that services the interests of all participants in the sport. Each of the four specialist climbing periodicals carries information on how to join the BMC.

Recommended reading

Instructional texts

The Handbook of Climbing by Alan Fyffe and Iain Peter (Pelham Books)
Mountaineering – The Freedom of the Hills edited by Ed Peters (The Mountaineers' Books)
A Manual of Modern Rope Techniques by Nigel Shepherd (Constable)
Climbing Fit by Martin Hurn and Pat Ingle (Crowood Press)
Modern Rock and Ice Climbing by Bill Birkett (A & C Black)

Inspirational reading

Games Climbers Play edited by Ken Wilson (Diadem)
Mirrors in the Cliffs edited by Jim Perrin (Diadem)
Classic Rock edited by Ken Wilson (Granada)
Hard Rock edited by Ken Wilson (Granada/Diadem)

Extreme Rock edited by Ken Wilson & Bernard Newman (Diadem)
Native Stones by David Craig (Secker and Warburg)
Rocks Around The World by Stefan Glowacz & Uli Weismeier (Diadem)
On and Off the Rocks by Jim Perrin (Gollancz)
Women Climbing by Bill Birkett & Bill Peascod (A & C Black)

Climbing magazines

Climber and Hillwalker (monthly)
Mountain (bi-monthly)
High (monthly), including the Journal of the British Mountaineering Council)
On The Edge (bi-monthly)

Glossary

Here is a selection of terms with specific meanings within the world of climbing.

Abseil (also **rappel, rap**) Method of descending a crag using a rope.

Aid Using a runner, or other piece of gear, to gain height on the rock; it is basically regarded as cheating, except during an *epic*.

Arête A prow of rock sticking outwards like the corner of a house.

Artificial or aid climbing Method of climbing holdless terrain by means of mechanical aids (e.g. pegs, nuts). It is virtually redundant in Britain, but is still important on *big walls* abroad.

Belay Stopping place with anchors, allowing the climber to be securely attached to the crag. It is also used to describe the act of holding the rope safely through a belay device.

'Below' Standard shouted warning of falling rocks, equipment, climbers, etc.

Big walls Climbs that take routes up huge rock-faces, often involving more than one day to climb. Virtually all such routes lie outside the British Isles.

Bivouac (often shortened to **bivvy**) To spend the night out without cover. It is common on *big walls* where ledges often provide the accommodation.

Bolt A permanent anchor occasionally used in areas of blank rock. A hole is drilled, and an expanding bolt is inserted. The use of bolts is considered totally unethical in the vast majority of British climbing areas.

Bombproof Substantial and safe runner or belay placement. It is often a welcome find.

Buttress A specific and well defined section of a crag.

Calls Regularly used communication between partners which are designed to reduce confusion.

Chalk A powder, light magnesium carbonate, used to dry the sweat from a climber's hands and fingers. It was once considered a form of cheating.

Chimney A cleft in the rock, large enough for a climber to enter and climb up on the inside.

Chockstone A stone firmly wedged in a crack, often providing a convenient runner or belay. *Artificial chockstone* is the original name for nut runners.

Choss Very poor quality or dirty rock.

Club hut Many climbing clubs own huts that are used by their members, and often other guests, as cheap accommodation in climbing areas.

Competitions A recent development in Britain, now confined to indoor walls, which allows climbers to compete directly with one another.

Corner A meeting of two rock walls in the manner of the inside of a half-open book.

Crux The most difficult section of a climb.

Descendeur Device which creates enough friction as the rope slides through it to provide a controlled descent for an abseiling climber.

Dogging Fashionable term for cheating on a climb by hanging on the runners in order to rest, while learning all the moves required. This activity was formerly called *French Style* climbing.

Epic Situation in which the ascent of a climb starts to get out of hand, often through inclement weather, lack of ability, lack of nerve and the growing realisation of having bitten off more than one can chew! It provides the substance for many tall tales related at a later date.

Ethics Set of unwritten rules that define the style of ascent considered proper by the current generation of climbers.

Free climbing Ascending a climb without resort to *aids* or other methods of cheating.

Friends Brand name of a device which uses the principles of camming to provide a reasonable runner in parallel-sided cracks; many other camming devices are now on the market.

Grades The suggested degree of difficulty of a climb, as recorded in guide books.

Gripped Descriptive term for a frightened climber; frequently occurs during an *epic*.

Harness Secure attachment to the rope (most often a sit-harness in Britain), made from *tape*, and consists of a combination of waist-belt and leg-loops.

Jamming Technique used to climb cracks by wedging fingers, hands or feet inside the crack.

Jug (shortened from 'jug-handle') A large hold.

Knots A large number exist, but there is little that cannot be achieved by the usual three: figure-of-eight, clove hitch

and double fisherman's.

Krab (short for 'karabiner') A snaplink used to join together ropes and tapes, preventing nylon running on nylon and thus melting. Screw-gate karabiners have a locking device to prevent accidental opening of the gate; snap-gates do not have one.

Line Thin rope made in the same way as climbing ropes and used to make loops for *nuts* or other runners.

Micro-wires Very small wired *nuts*, often made from a brass alloy, which provide runners where none were previously possible.

Nuts Aluminium wedges, or other shapes, inserted by hand into cracks to provide runners or belays. They are removed after use to leave the rock as it was found.

On-sight The ideal. To ascend a climb or new route with no prior knowledge or inspection.

PAs Original rock boots named after their creator Pierre Allain; the term is still used as a general description of climbing footwear.

Peg Metal spike, or piton, hammered into a crack in the rock to provide a runner or belay where no other alterna-

tive exists.

Prusik Knot tied onto climbing rope with a thin line sling and used to ascend the rope.

Quick-draw (formerly 'tie-off' or 'extender') Term describing the short tape connector between two krabs, used for connecting *wires* or *bolts* to the climbing rope.

Rack Selection of gear carried by a climber leading a pitch.

Red-point Ascent in good style of a *sport climb*, usually after considerable practice.

Rocks Brand of wedge-shaped *nuts* that has become a generic term for that particular shape.

Runner Short for 'running belay' used to protect the climber who is leading. It is also used to describe the individual anchors of a belay.

Sling A loop of rope or (more usually) tape, either knotted or sewn, and used as a runner over spikes, around threads or as an extender to prevent rope drag when leading.

Solo climbing Climber attempting a route without the safeguard of rope, runners or partners. It is obviously more dangerous, but can be very satisfying . . .

if completed!

Sport climbing Climbs created under European influence, and on which runners are provided almost totally by bolts; the climbs are thus simply gymnastic problems with no involvement of risk or adventure.

Sticht plate Brand name, now used generically, of original belay plate.

Stickies Name usually applied to the modern generation of very sticky rubber-soled climbing boots or shoes.

Tape Nylon woven into a flat, and often very strong, tape. It is used to make harnesses and slings.

Thin Difficult climbing on small holds.

Top rope Method of ropework that involves protecting the climber by means of a rope belayed at the top of the crag.

UIAA International Union of Alpine Associations. It is known mainly for the safety standards it has applied to climbing equipment. (From 1992 all climbing gear will be subject to European CEN standards which will ensure minimum specifications for every type of safety equipment.)

Wires Smaller sized *nuts* threaded with a braided wire loop for strength.

First aid

In addition to the moral responsibility of everyone to know a little first aid, first aid training should be regarded as essential in preparing to partake in a risk sport such as rock climbing. Even a basic course will impart the knowledge that may save a friend's life.

Disclaimer

Rock climbing is a potentially dangerous sport. Whilst every effort has been made to demonstrate safe practice, neither the author nor publisher can accept any responsibility for the application of the information contained in this text or for the actions of any individual subsequent to its consultation.

◀ *Another finger jam, this time used thumb-up*

Index

Starting a serious abseil in the south ▶
of France

)